SAGUARO NATIONAL PARK

A TRUE BOOK

by
David Petersen

Children's Press®
A Division of Grolier Publishing
New York London Hong Kong Sydney
Danbury, Connecticut

A bat lands on a saguaro flower

Subject Consultant
Tom Danton
Chief of Interpretation
Saguaro National Park

Reading Consultant
Linda Cornwell
Coordinator of School Quality
and Improvement
Indiana State Teachers
Association

**Visit Children's Press® on the
Internet at:
http://publishing.grolier.com**

Library of Congress Cataloging-in-Publication Data

Petersen, David, 1946-.
  Saguaro National Park / by David Petersen.
    p.   cm. — (A true book)
  Includes bibliographical references and index.
  Summary: Describes the history, landscape, wildlife, and activities
available for visitors at Saguaro National Park.
    ISBN: 0-516-20944-2 (lib. bdg.)   0-516-26771-X (pbk.)
    1.Saguaro National Park (Ariz.)—Juvenile literature. [1. Saguaro
National Park (Ariz.) 2. National parks.] I. Title. II. Series.
F817.S18P48   1999
917.91′77—dc21   98-28806
                                                                 CIP
                                                                  AC

Contents

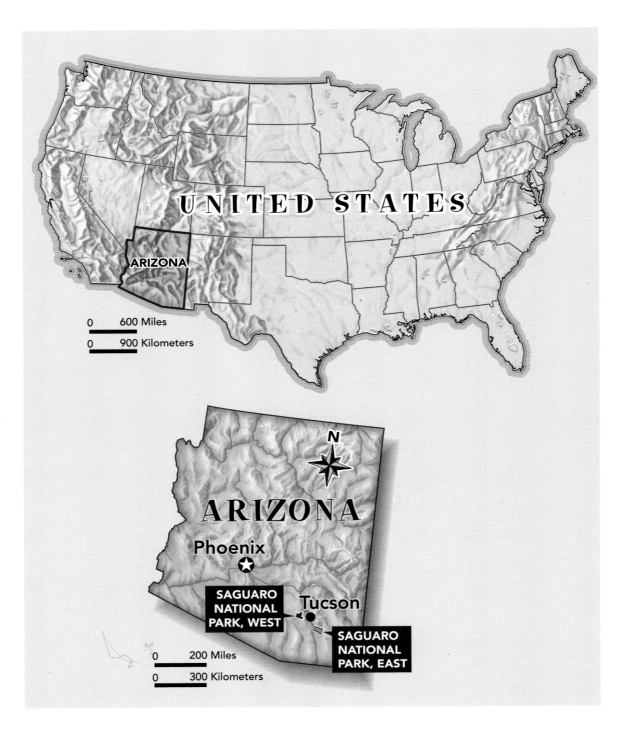

Desert Magic

Everywhere you look in nature—the sky, the water, the forests and fields—there is living magic. And the deserts are among nature's most magical places.

Of North America's four great deserts, the liveliest is the Sonoran (suh-NOR-an).

Most of the Sonoran lies south of the United States border, in Mexico. But part of it pokes north into southern Arizona. It abounds in wild plants, wild creatures—and in natural beauty.

The Sonoran Desert's lively green beauty is made possible by mild winters and two rainy seasons a year. Winter rains fall gently over large areas. Summer rains appear as brief, violent thunderstorms.

Lightning highlights a saguaro cactus.

The sandy desert soil dries quickly. But the summer and winter rains provide enough moisture to support about 2,700 species, or kinds, of trees, bushes, and wildflowers, and fifty kinds of cacti (the

An ocotillo cactus in bloom

plural of cactus) that thrive in dry soil.

Many animals also make the Sonoran Desert their home. These include deer, coyotes, rabbits, rodents, bobcats, birds, and lots of snakes and lizards. Among the more unusual

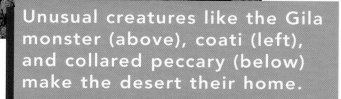

Unusual creatures like the Gila monster (above), coati (left), and collared peccary (below) make the desert their home.

Sonoran animals are a raccoon-like creature called the coati (co-AH-tee), a big, colorful lizard called the Gila (HEE-la) monster, and the piglike collared peccary (PE-kah-ree).

In an average year, the Sonoran Desert receives only about 11 inches (28 centimeters) of rain. In summer, temperatures rise above 100 degrees Fahrenheit (38 degrees Celsius) nearly every day, sometimes soaring to 120° F (49° C)! While Sonoran life is abundant, it is never easy.

Sonoran Life

To avoid the midday summer heat, and to reduce their need for water, most Sonoran animals nap in the shade of plants or rocks. Some animals burrow underground. In the evening, as the air and ground cool, animals emerge, or come out, to eat, drink, and move

In the cool of evening, prairie dogs come out.

around. So even though the desert may appear to be dead in the daytime, it hops, jumps, and crawls with life at night.

The organ pipe cactus and yellow palo verde tree live side by side.

Like the animals, desert plants must adapt to the extreme heat and dryness of their home. Sonoran trees, such as the mesquite and palo verde, reduce their water needs by staying small. Deep roots find water far below the desert's surface.

Sonoran wildflowers include marigolds, asters, lupines, and many more. These flowers avoid summer's wilting heat and drought by blooming in the spring. This is when the air is cool and the soil is still damp from winter rains.

A carpet of wildflowers is a surprise you may find in the desert.

But the plants most at home in the desert are the cacti. And the king of all cacti is the giant, many-armed saguaro (sa-WAHR-o).

Saguaro—Desert Monarch

From a seed smaller than a grain of sand, across a two-hundred-year lifetime, a saguaro can grow as tall as a five-story building. It can weigh as much as 16,000 pounds (7,273 kilograms). To support this massive weight,

The mighty saguaro cactus can be taller than your home or school.

The internal ribs
of a dead cactus

the saguaro has a strong
skeleton of woody ribs.

Like other cacti, everything
about the saguaro is designed
to gather, store, and conserve
water. From a single soaking

rain, a saguaro's wide, shallow root system can absorb 200 gallons (757 liters) of water— a full year's supply!

To store all that liquid, the saguaro has thick, spongy flesh. Pleats on its surface expand like an accordion, allowing the plant to grow as it soaks up water. Meaty branches, called arms, provide additional water storage. A smooth, waxy skin reflects the sun's heat and seals moisture

Ouch! Here's a close look at saguaro cactus needles.

inside. Long, sharp needles protect the juicy plant from being eaten by animals.

Yet, in spite of its thorns, many birds and insects call the saguaro home. Hawks build nests in saguaro arms. Nest

A Harris hawk (above) and an elf owl (left) make cozy nests in the saguaro cactus.

holes drilled into saguaros by woodpeckers provide cool, safe "apartments" for wrens, warblers, falcons, martins, and owls.

Saguaro

Each May, mature saguaros blossom with big white flowers. The honeylike nectar in these flowers attracts bees, bats, and birds. By traveling from one saguaro to another, these flying animals fertilize the flowers, allowing fruit to grow.

In June and July, big red saguaro fruits appear where

Fruit

the flowers had been. When these fruits ripen, they are eagerly eaten by insects, animals—and people. Tohono O'Odham (TOH-na OH-tahm) Indians, Sonoran Desert natives, use long poles made of saguaro ribs to gather the fruits.

The sweet, seedy, juicy fruits are used in syrups, jams, and wine, or are dried and eaten like figs.

For thousands of years, human and animal natives of the Sonoran Desert lived in harmony with the saguaro. Then, in the late 1800s, white settlers came pouring in. And with them, they brought cattle.

Grazing among the saguaro, the clumsy cattle trampled young cacti and packed the soil so that seeds could not sprout. Before grazing was ended a hundred years later, some saguaro forests had been

Travelers in the 1890s make a stop downtown on their way to settle Sonoran land.

destroyed. Many others were badly damaged.

To protect America's precious treasure of saguaros from destruction, Congress established Saguaro National

0   100 Miles

0   150 Kilometers

N

ARIZONA

Phoenix ★

SAGUARO NATIONAL PARK, WEST

SAGUARO NATIONAL PARK, EAST

Tucson

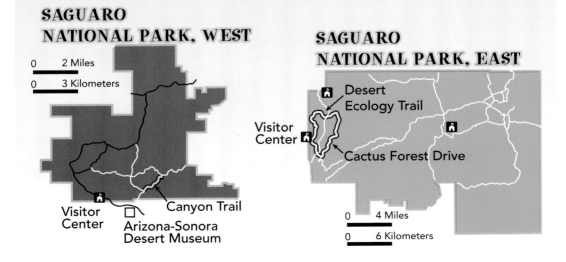

SAGUARO NATIONAL PARK, WEST

0   2 Miles

0   3 Kilometers

Visitor Center

Arizona-Sonora Desert Museum

Canyon Trail

SAGUARO NATIONAL PARK, EAST

Desert Ecology Trail

Visitor Center

Cactus Forest Drive

0   4 Miles

0   6 Kilometers

Monument, near Tucson, Arizona, in 1933.

Recently, the monument became Saguaro National Park. Saguaro National Park is actually made up of two parks that are 30 miles (48 kilometers) apart. One is located 15 miles (24 km) east of Tucson. The other is located 15 miles (24 km) west of the city. Together, these two parks protect 91,327 acres (36,975 hectares) of Sonoran Desert life and landscapes.

Saguaro East— Rincon Mountain District

Saguaro East is the larger of the two parks. It rises from the cactus-studded desert floor, up through brushy foothills, to the high forested peaks of the Rincon Mountains. Nearly 130 miles (209 km) of foot and horse

The teddybear cholla (above) and the prickly pear cactus (right)

trails loop high and low
throughout the park.
Down on the desert floor it
is hot, dry, and prickly. In

addition to thousands of saguaros, you will see many smaller species of cacti, including barrel, hedgehog, fish-hook, and prickly pear. Most of these you can touch—if you are careful.

But one Sonoran cactus you should avoid is the teddybear cholla (COY-yuh). Also called jumping cholla, its spiny pods break off easily, and can attach fiercely to your skin. The cholla's needles are barbed, hard to remove, and very painful.

One tiny bird, the cactus wren, has learned to use the cholla to its advantage. By nesting within the prickly plant, the wren and its young are well protected from predators.

A cactus wren finds a safe place to rest in a cholla.

The Gila woodpecker feeds on the nectar of flowers throughout the desert.

In fact, Saguaro National Park is alive with bright, colorful birds and their cheerful songs: quail, warblers, woodpeckers, thrashers, doves, elf owls, kingbirds, kestrels, and more.

A great place to start your tour of Saguaro East is the visitor center. There you will find plant, animal, and geology displays that you can look at and touch. You will also find slide and video programs, friendly rangers, and guided nature walks.

Park rangers share their knowledge about desert animal and plant life.

Next, hop in the car for a driving tour through the heart of the saguaro forest, following the 8-mile (13-km) cactus forest scenic drive. If you're hungry, stop for lunch at one of the two picnic areas.

And be sure to stroll the Desert Ecology Trail. Signs along this scenic path identify native plants and animals and explain the importance of water in the desert.

Ponderosa pine trees are found in the Rincon Mountains.

Climbing above the desert floor and into the foothills, the scenery begins to change. Saguaros are replaced by brush and small trees. Near the tops of the Rincon Mountains, you will enter cool, shady groves of

The city of Tucson, with the Rincons in the distance

Douglas fir and giant ponderosa pine trees. Deer and even bears live here. From the high Rincons, you can gaze down onto Saguaro East, out across sprawling Tucson, all the way to Saguaro West.

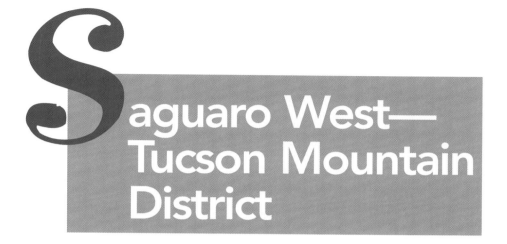

Saguaro West—Tucson Mountain District

Beginning at the Red Hills visitor center, the Bajada Loop Drive winds 9 miles (15 km) through rolling, rocky hills covered with saguaro cacti. These cacti look like thousands of big green people waving their arms. Stop for a picnic if you

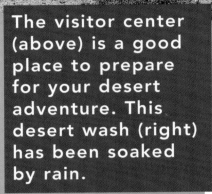

The visitor center (above) is a good place to prepare for your desert adventure. This desert wash (right) has been soaked by rain.

like. And be sure to explore one or more of the big sandy washes.

A wash is a desert stream-bed that is dry except after heavy rains, when flash floods come roaring down from the rocky hills. Thick vegetation trims most washes, providing food and shelter for wildlife. Washes are wonderful places to spot wild animals—especially in the cool, shady minutes just after daylight and just before dark. And desert washes make great natural playgrounds, where you can

The coyote and the black-tailed jackrabbit have adapted well to the desert environment.

run and jump and dig in the sand and explore all the wild mysteries waiting just around the bend.

Before leaving Saguaro West, you'll want to visit the nearby Arizona-Sonoran Desert Museum. With its collection of

A unique learning experience awaits you at the Arizona-Sonoran Desert Museum.

three hundred kinds of plants and two hundred species of animals, this is one of the finest "living museums" in the world. It is huge, so allow a full fun day to enjoy it.

Your Saguaro Adventure

There are few places like Saguaro National Park—with its sandy winding washes, its odd creatures, and its beauty, mystery, and magic. Best of all, Saguaro National Park is home to America's grandest cactus. There, the monarch of the Sonoran

The beauty of the Saguaro Desert attracts visitors year round.

Desert is waiting to meet you, its arms open wide.

To Find Out More

Here are some additional resources to help you learn more about Saguaro National Park:

Books

Bailey, Donna. **Lizards.** Raintree Steck-Vaughn, 1992.

Fradin, Dennis B. **Arizona.** Children's Press, 1993.

George, Michael. **Birds.** Child's World, 1991.

Jernigan, E. Wesley. **Sonoran Seasons: A Year in the Desert.** Harbinger House, 1994.

Storad, Conrad J. **Saguaro Cactus.** Lerner Publications, 1994.

Wright-Frierson, Virginia. **Desert Scrapbook: Dawn to Dusk in the Sonoran Desert.** Simon and Schuster, 1996.

Organizations and Online Sites

Arizona-Sonoran Desert Museum
2021 North Kinney Road
Tucson, AZ 85743
http://desert.net/museum/ exhibits.htmlx

Enter a virtual cave to explore the museum's mineral collection. There are also "cool stuff you'll see" listings for animals, plants, and insects.

National Park Service
Office of Public Inquiries
P.O. Box 37127
Washington, D.C. 20240
http://www.nps.gov

General information on all the national parks.

Saguaro National Park
3693 South Old
  Spanish Trail
Tucson, AZ 85730
http://www.desertusa.com/ sag/du_sag_index.html

Facts on desert life, a calendar of activities at the park, an online store, and a Desert News Flash department updated each month.

Sonoran Desert Naturalist
http://members.aol.com/ Melasoma/index.html

Tales about Sonoran birds, plants, and insects, wildflower reports, and lots of links to related sites.

Important Words

adapt to change according to need

cacti desert plants that have spines instead of leaves

drought a long, dry time without rain or snow

ecology a natural community, including plants, animals, and landscapes

geology the study of Earth's history and features

monarch a king, queen, or other ruler

predator an animal that hunts, kills, and eats other animals in order to survive

wash the dry bed of a stream

Index

Meet the Author

David Petersen lives in the Rocky Mountains of Colorado. He and his wife, Caroline, visit Saguaro National Park every spring, when the wildflowers are blooming. David has written many True Books on America's national parks (*Bryce Canyon, Denali, Death Valley, Petrified Forest,* and others), as well as the True Book Continents series. He is the author of many books about the natural world, for adults as well as children, including *Elkheart: A Personal Tribute to Wapiti and Their World* (Boulder, CO: Johnson Books, 1998).